Amsterdam

Amsterdam

Photos: Jan den Hengst

Text: Jacques Constant

inmerc bv, Wormer

Contents

6 Central Station
8 Exchange and finance
10 Dam and palace
12 From post office to shopping centre
14 The smell of tar and ropes
16 Montelbaanstoren and surrounds
18 Life in the 17th century
22 Housing in the 'twenties
24 Life after the 'eighties
28 Living on and near water
30 The University of Amsterdam
32 Hotels on historic sites
34 A sea of flowers
36 The Magere Brug area
38 Art and Administration under one roof
40 Rummaging in the Waterlooplein market
42 Jewish History Museum
44 Anne Frank house
46 Renzo Piano's 'shipwreck'
48 Sail Amsterdam
50 Nature in miniature
52 The piety of the merchant
54 The oasis of the pious women
56 History of a city
60 Eating and drinking
64 Temple to Lady Fortune
66 Musical extremes
68 The Rijksmuseum
76 The past for sale
78 Advertising from centuries ago
80 Markets of Amsterdam
82 Vincent van Gogh in Amsterdam
84 Modern art behind old walls
86 Amsterdam and water
88 Public transport
90 Bank as fairy-tale palace
92 Spaceship for Ajax Amsterdam
94 Schiphol

Amsterdam

Amsterdam – capital and financial centre of the Netherlands – is a special city. You can come across all of the city's main sights and attractions simply by walking or cycling: the Royal Palace and Madame Tussaud's on the same square, behind the palace a modern shopping centre in a 19th-century post office, the flea market next to the city hall and opera house, museums of ancient and modern art within a few paces of one another, the best international cuisine. This book looks at all these opposites, as a memento of the city of Rembrandt with a museum for Vincent van Gogh. Or as a guide when visiting the city of the world-famous Royal Concertgebouw Orchestra and the equally renowned barrel organ.

The main entrance to the Central Station is richly decorated with allegorical reliefs. This neo-Renaissance extravaganza was designed by the architect P. J. H. Cuypers and built between 1882 and 1889. The ornamentation of the façade is repeated inside, notably in the restaurant on Platform 1, which used to be the first-class waiting room.

In front of the Central Station is a picturesque wooden coffee-house. It has a large terrace where round-trip boats can moor and also houses a VVV (tourist information) office.

Central Station

For many visitors, the Central Station is the gateway to Amsterdam. Trams, buses and Metro trains leave from the square in front of it to all parts of the city and beyond. It was built at the end of the 19th century on a man-made island between the River IJ and the city's harbour front. Previously, ships left for the farthest corners of the world from the quay opposite the main entrance. Many of the buildings on this quay are reminiscent of those times, especially the Schreierstoren (Weepers Tower). This squat 15th-century fortification was so named because it was where the sailors' wives saw the ships off on voyages which could last for years, or where they waited in vain for their husbands' return. The imposing church behind the Schreierstoren is also a reminder of the city's maritime past. It was completed in 1887 and dedicated to St. Nicholas, the patron saint of sailors.

The former harbour front of Amsterdam, opposite the Central Station, was permanently cut off from the sea by the construction of the railway terminus. In the middle is the medieval Schreierstoren and, beyond it, the neo-Baroque St.-Nicolaaskerk. The majority of the façades pre-date the station. This small section of the former harbour now offers moorage for round-trip boats, water taxis and pedalos.

Exchange and finance

Amsterdam's hey-day began at the end of the 16th century. Until that time it had been a city of small tradesmen and artisans. Dozens of ornamental wall plaques in the old centre still bear witness to their activities. In 1585, after the Spanish captured Antwerp, then the commercial capital of Western Europe, many merchants fled to Amsterdam. Their arrival led not only to a rapid expansion of overseas trade, but turned the city into a financial centre of international importance. It remained so for several centuries. Architectural reminders of this chapter in Amsterdam's history stand in the Beursplein (Exchange Square). The present-day Amsterdam Stock Exchange is located here, in addition to the Commodities Exchange built between 1889 and 1903 by the architect H. P. Berlage. He broke away from the popular revivalist styles, of which the Central Station is a good example, and produced a design that was new and revolutionary. The Commodities Exchange has been used as an exhibition centre and concert hall since the late 1980s.

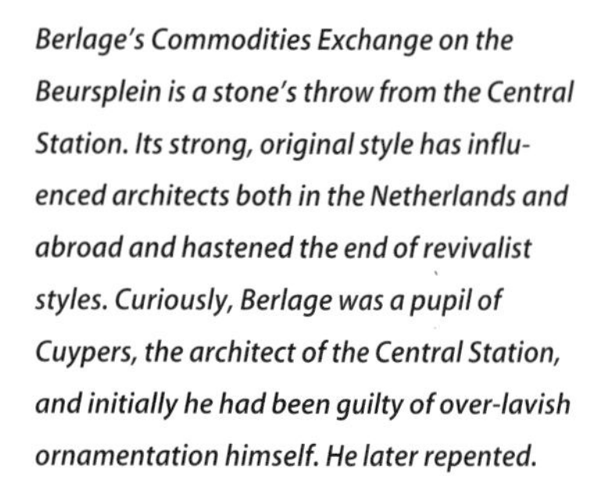

Berlage's Commodities Exchange on the Beursplein is a stone's throw from the Central Station. Its strong, original style has influenced architects both in the Netherlands and abroad and hastened the end of revivalist styles. Curiously, Berlage was a pupil of Cuypers, the architect of the Central Station, and initially he had been guilty of over-lavish ornamentation himself. He later repented.

Preserved ornamental wall plaques recall two of the trades which once flourished in the city. The one dated 1626 advertises a grain merchant's delivery services, the other suggests that a brewery existed on the site.

The Amsterdam Stock Exchange shares the Beursplein with Berlage's Commodities Exchange. The decline of trading in the Commodities Exchange is due to the introduction of computerized trading in the stock market.

BEIDT UW TYD
BEURS VAN BERLAGE
EEN
fantastische
HEMELREIS
28/06 – 31/08
BEURSPLEIN
BEURSPLEIN

The Dam and the surrounding neighbourhood forms a stage for all kinds of street artists, from living statues to musicians and acrobats. Every once in a while, they (and the pigeons) have to make way for a large fair. A regular fixture is the traditional Koninginnedag (Queen's Day), held on 30th April.

Four major shopping streets end at the Dam: Kalverstraat, Nieuwendijk, Rokin and Damrak. Kalverstraat and Nieuwendijk are best known for their clothes shops, Rokin for its art and antique shops. The Bijenkorf department store looks out on to the Damrak, which leads to the Central Station; its window displays are often minor artistic masterpieces, particularly at Christmas.

The Dam is dominated by the Koninklijh Paleis (Royal Palace), built in the 17th century to a design by the architect Jacob van Campen. It was originally the town hall for a rich and powerful Amsterdam and did not become a palace until Napoleon's younger brother Louis was crowned King of Holland and moved into it in 1808. The French departed in 1813 and, the following year, when the House of Orange took over, they kept it as a palace. Now it is open to the public, except when the royal banner indicates that Queen Beatrix is present for an official reception.

Dam and palace

The Dam is the teeming heart of the Dutch capital. Originally built to stop storm-waters flooding in from the north, it now swarms with Amsterdam shoppers, tourists and hurried business people – as well as thousands of pigeons which will eat out of your hand. The birds have settled in the buildings surrounding the square, including the Koninklijk Paleis (Royal Palace), the Nieuwe Kerk (New Church), Madame Tussaud's Wax Museum and a number of large shops and department stores. Street artists, musicians, preachers and ice-cream vendors do their bit to enliven the atmosphere, and every once in a while the square is taken over by demonstrators, of which Amsterdam has plenty.

The Nieuwe Kerk (New Church) stands next to the palace. Construction of this Gothic building began in the 14th century, but the tower was never completed. The church contains the tomb of Michiel de Ruyter, the Dutch admiral who was the bane of the English in the 17th century. Nowadays, it is mainly used for exhibitions.

From post office to shopping centre

Behind the Koninklijk Paleis is a building as remarkable as it is excessive. The Government Architect C. H. Peters designed it as a post office at the end of the 19th century. He was inspired by the Renaissance chancellery in Leeuwarden in Friesland, but could not resist adding elements from various other styles. After all, it was his most substantial creation and he was going to make sure that everyone in the Netherlands knew about it! The people of Amsterdam, never at a loss for a nickname, quickly termed the brick colossus 'the Pear Castle', after the shape of the cupolas on top of the towers. The PTT (Dutch Post Office and Telecommunications Company) left the building in the late 1980s. After a thorough overhaul, it was reopened in 1992 as a luxurious shopping centre called Magna Plaza. Around the galleried central courtyard are three floors of shops selling exclusive clothes and gift items. One of the largest music stores in Amsterdam is located in the basement.

The great hall, where the post office counters used to be, has remained more or less unchanged. The offices in the arcades, however, have been divided up and converted into dozens of boutiques. To reach the upper floors, if the mood takes you, you can try your luck and climb the rope bridge – or you could take the escalator.

The 'Pear Castle' on Nieuwezijds Voorburgwal is large, imposing and a good example of the revivalist styles popular in Western Europe at the end of the 19th century. Despite its transformation from a post office into a shopping centre, much of its overwhelming diversity of colours and shapes has survived inside as well as out.

For a number of years, the Amsterdam has been moored next to the Maritime Museum. It is a replica of a Dutch East India Company ship that left in 1749 for the East loaded with cargo, office supplies and ballast. However, it did not get very far. While still in the North Sea, the Amsterdam encountered a heavy storm and sank soon afterwards off the English coast near Hastings. The replica is based on old drawings and studies of the wreck. Although it cannot sail, it has been authentically fitted out complete with navigational instruments of the time. An 18th-century sailor's life is acted out on board and a ship's cook prepares the food on which the crew would have had to survive.

The Maritime Museum is housed in a dour, virtually square building east of the Central Station. In the 17th century, it was 's Lands Zeemagazijn: a warehouse where the Admiralty of Amsterdam kept a supply of just about everything necessary for their war fleet, from ropes and sails and compasses to weapons and

ammunition. Further along Oostenburgergracht, the Dutch East India Company (Verenigde Oost-Indische Compagnie, or VOC for short) – which had the Dutch monopoly on trade with South-East Asia, especially present-day Indonesia – built a shipyard and a rope walk. In 1697, Tsar Peter the Great of Russia trained there as a ship's carpenter.

The smell of tar and ropes

In the mid-17th century, the Republic of the United Netherlands developed into one of the most important seafaring nations in Europe. Competition with England made a strong navy essential, but because the Republic was a federation of provinces, control of the fleet was divided between five admiralties. The most powerful was the Admiralty of Amsterdam, which therefore took the lead in fitting out and provisioning the warships. In 1655, just after the first Anglo-Dutch war, the Admiralty had a maritime warehouse with an adjoining shipyard built in nine months on three artificial islands on a marshy section of the IJ. This warehouse, with an area of 63 x 57 metres, has housed the Nederlands Scheepvaartmuseum (Dutch Maritime Museum) since 1973. The extensive collection includes the Royal Barge built in 1818 and used by the royal family until 1962.

Montelbaanstoren and surrounds

The Montelbaanstoren (Montelbaan Tower) is on Oudeschans, not far from the Scheepvaartmuseum. It looks rather like a church, but that is because a frivolous spire was added at the start of the 17th century. The much more staid section below the spire, dating from 1512, was a truncated tower with a platform for cannons. It formed part of the defensive works on Oudeschans. At one point in the 19th century, the Montelbaanstoren came very close to destruction when the city council decided it was an obstacle and prepared to demolish it. Even the argument that the clock on the tower was essential for the local residents made no impression on the councillors. However, the demolition plans were halted at the last minute. Today, the tower houses the City Water Offices, which – among other things – monitor the water level in Amsterdam's canals. The surrounding area is renowned not only for its picturesque canals – the city's oldest – but also for its many merchant's houses and warehouses.

The Montelbaanstoren stands on the corner of Oude Waal and Oudeschans. The lower section dates from the 16th century and formed part of Amsterdam's fortifications. The octagonal superstructure and wooden tower were added in the 17th century.

Windmills stood on almost every dike in Amsterdam in the 17th century. When the ramparts were demolished, all but two of them were lost. One is De Gooyer, on Funen, within walking distance of the Scheepvaartmuseum. At its base, a traditional brewery opened some years ago in the former public baths. It brews its own special sort of beer which is quite different from the usual brands produced by the large Dutch breweries.

The West-Indisch Huis (West India House) is on Haarlemmerstraat, fifteen minutes' walk from the Scheepvaartmuseum. It was once the headquarters of the Dutch West India Company (WIC), established in 1622. This association was given the Dutch monopoly on trade and shipping to America. It was in this building that the far-reaching decision was taken, in 1625, to establish the city of New Amsterdam, now known as New York. The Oost-Indisch Huis (East India House) is located on Oude Hoogstraat. The Dutch East India Company, which had its headquarters there, was considerably more powerful than the WIC.

Life in the 17th century

If you want to see how Amsterdam's aristocracy used to live, visit the Museum van Loon at Keizersgracht 672. Built in classical style, the house is staid and sober on the outside; the only decorations are four reliefs of Roman gods on the wall. Two of these – Mars, the god of war, and Vulcan, the god of fire – represent the business interests of the arms dealer and iron-master, Jeremias van Raey, who built this canal-side house and the building next door in the second half of the 17th century. Once inside, visitors are overwhelmed by the wealth of furniture, household goods and decorations that whisk them back to Amsterdam's Golden Age. The interior has been maintained intact thanks to Maurits van Loon, a descendant of the aristocratic Amsterdam family that acquired the house at the end of the 19th century and lived in it until the 1960s. He had the house completely restored between 1964 and 1973.

The carefully restored house has two floors open to the public. The interior and furniture date mainly from the 17th and 18th centuries. The intricate wrought-iron banisters of the staircase contain the words VHAGEN and TRIP. These are the names of Doctor Abraham van Hagen, who bought the house in 1752, and the mayor's daughter, Catharina Trip, a patient of Van Hagen's whom he later married.

Behind the Museum van Loon is a beautiful geometric garden which, like the house, has also been restored to its original condition. At the end of the garden is a coach house built in the style of a classical temple.

It is hardly surprising that Jeremias van Raey, the original owner, chose to build on Keizersgracht. Of the four canals built in a semi-circle around the medieval city centre, Keizersgracht is the most distinguished. It was named after Kaiser Maximilian, Archduke of Austria, who granted Amsterdam the privilege of including his crown in its coat of arms.

The house and its furnishings perfectly match the luxurious lifestyle of the aristocratic Van Loon family at the beginning of the 20th century. The servants wore black livery and Lady Thora van Loon was famous for her receptions, known as 'jours'. She was lady-in-waiting to Queen Wilhelmina (1880-1962) and often travelled to the palace in one of the family's seven coaches. The coach house in the garden was too small to accommodate all of them, so they were kept in a building on the other side of the canal.

Around 50 portraits, from 17th-century paintings to photographs from the 1920s, commemorate the aristocratic families that lived in this house. One portrait that is missing is of Ferdinand Bol, a student of Rembrandt's. Bol rented the house for a number of years from the first owner, who lived at No. 674.

Housing in the Twenties

A backlash against the subdued architecture of Berlage's Commodities Exchange, built at the turn of the century, began after 1911. A number of architects attempted to introduce a wider and more imaginative palette of shapes and colours. They have become known as the Amsterdam School and made their mark on much of what was built in the city between the First and Second World Wars. Some of them were influenced by socialist ideals and set out to design decent housing for the workers. They were given the chance because it was precisely at this time that the city needed to build whole new residential neighbourhoods in a short space of time. One of the best examples of such a social housing complex, designed in one go, is in the Spaarndammerbuurt, about two kilometres from the Central Station.

This block of flats on Hembrugstraat has become the symbol of the Amsterdam School. Faced in brick, it is an elaborate composition of roofs, bay windows and a slim tower serving purely as decoration. The intention of the architect, Michel de Klerk, was to create a living environment that was better than the grey working-class slums of the late-19th century. However, the residents were not always totally happy with this type of housing. Many housewives – who, according to long-standing Dutch custom, were fanatical window cleaners – were driven mad by the many small window-panes.

This four-faced rounded tower connects two of the outer blocks of the complex in a harmonious manner. At its base is the entrance to a post office. Characteristic of the eccentric approach of the Amsterdam School is the tile-hung design used for the first-floor storeys either side of the tower.

The architects of the Amsterdam School treated the façade as a work of art and used it as a decorative surface. The intention was to hide the structure of the building as much as possible with brickwork and ornament. Occasionally an architect would design only the façade and leave the planning of the flats behind it to the contractor.

Like most of his colleagues, de Klerk let his imagination run wild with a variety of adornments that had no practical purpose. This corner bay extending over three floors is an example. From the outside it is charming; on the inside it is just big enough to accommodate a chair.

On Oudeschans, there is another example of the Amsterdam policy of filling holes with homes. Only die-hard moaners complain that the new block of flats, built of concrete but clad with grey aerated bricks, is out of keeping with the area. The social-democrat city council, when forced to defend its housing policies, had a sharp retort for its critics: "you can't live in bulls—t". In the background is the Montelbaanstoren.

The new buildings along the line of the Metro are connected with the rest of the old town by alleyways and vistas in as natural a manner as possible. Between two modern blocks the tower of the Zuiderkerk can be seen. Built at the beginning of the 17th century, it still has all but two of the 35 original bells cast by the famous bell foundry, Hemony's. The master builder, Hendrik de Keyser, is buried here in his own church.

On Amsterdam's canals people live not only in purpose-built houseboats but also in canal barges dating from the 19th and 20th centuries. Until a few years after the Second World War, living on houseboats was a necessity due to the shortage of housing. Nowadays, it has become a way of life. Many Amsterdammers prefer it, even though mooring charges have risen exorbitantly and life on canal barges is often pretty basic.

Living on and near water

In the distant past, travellers from abroad compared Amsterdam to Venice, in part because it was a centre of foreign trade, but primarily because it was dissected in every direction by canals. Even now, many Amsterdammers live on or next to the water. Canal-side houses are among the most expensive in the city. Houseboats are moored stem to stern, sometimes in double rows, on almost every canal. Some are hardly different, in terms of comfort or price, from the houses they look out on. Unlike Venice, however, Amsterdam is not restricted to water traffic. Even if the canals freeze over – which does happen in harsh winters – it causes few problems. The city council simply closes off a large number of canals to round-trip boats and other shipping and gives Amsterdammers a chance to cross the city on skates.

The University of Amsterdam

Like many universities with a long history, the University of Amsterdam is not housed in one large complex. Departments and faculties are spread throughout the city. The university developed from the Athenaeum Illustre, which opened in 1632. Until 1864 it was housed in the Agnietenkapel, a former 15th-century convent chapel. These days, students rarely enter the original building. Part of it is a museum of paintings, photographs, objects and documents showing university life since 1632. This, at least, is a more dignified use than the previous one: the chapel served for many years as a warehouse for the Admiralty of Amsterdam.

The Agnietenkapel is entered via the Agnietenpoortje (Agnieten Gate) on Oudezijds Voorburgwal. The gate did not originally belong to the chapel, but came from the former municipal carpenters' yard. The gilded figures above the entrance indicate the year in which the Athenaeum Illustre was founded, 1632, and the year the chapel was restored, 1921. At that time, the medieval convent chapel was fitted out as a lecture hall for the university.

Part of the Agnietenkapel houses a permanent exhibition containing a selection of the University of Amsterdam's historical collections.

Most departments of the University of Amsterdam are located in the old city centre. Some have spacious courtyards where students can enjoy the sun between lectures or revise for their exams.

The interior of the Doelen Hotel has been modernized a number of times since it was built in 1882/83. From the outside, however, the neo-classical building has lost none of its 19th-century elegance.

The Hotel de l'Europe was built in neo-Renaissance style, and is known above all for its stunning terrace on the Amstel.

Hotels on historic sites

In the second half of the 19th century, the completion of the railways created a new travelling public, wealthy, numerous and in search of first-class comfort on and off the trains. In many European cities, a new type of accommodation was appearing to meet the demand: the grand hotel. It looked like a palace and was intended to impress with its luxury and prestige. Amsterdam still has a number of these palatial establishments. Two, the Doelen Hotel and the Hotel de l'Europe, are close to Muntplein. This junction of tramlines is dominated by the Munttoren (Mint Tower), in which coins were struck for many years during the 17th century. The Hotel de l'Europe is built on the site of a 16th-century fortification, the Rondeel (Roundel). The Doelen Hotel stands on the former parade ground of the Kloveniersgilde, the musketeer branch of the civic militia. In 1638, the board of the guild commissioned Rembrandt to paint the company of Captain Frans Banning Cocq. The resulting canvas is better known as the *Night Watch*.

Guests at the Hotel de l'Europe look out over the busy Muntplein junction and the Munttoren with its carillon. Until the 17th century the base of the tower formed part of the city's medieval fortifications. The rest of the Muntplein lay outside the city walls and was known as the Ossenmarkt (Ox Market).

A SEA OF FLOWERS

The Netherlands has been famous for its flowers ever since the tulip mania of the early 17th century, when fortunes were made and lost as speculators bid up the price of the rarest bulbs to unsustainable peaks. Later, the growing of tulips, hyacinths and other blooms which flourish in the sandy soils around Haarlem settled down and became a serious industry. Today the country is the largest flower exporter in the world. There are even plans to build a tunnel between Amsterdam airport and the huge flower auction at Aalsmeer to make the exporting of flowers easier. In Amsterdam, the main place to find flowers is the famous flower market on the Singel, behind the Munttoren. Even in winter, the market is a sea of cut flowers and flowering plants. Some overflow into the street, others can be found in covered stalls on boats in the canal. The market on the Singel is not the only flower market in the city, but it is the best known. Foreign visitors cluster to buy bulbs there as a memento of the vibrant colours with which Amsterdammers like to brighten their northern skies.

Wherever you find tourists in the Netherlands, you will also find clogs. Very few Dutch people still wear them, but foreigners keep buying them, hence the huge pair in front of a souvenir shop in the flower market. Though pure fantasy, the decoration is another reminder of the Dutch love of colourful embellishment – and the clogs make a nice snapshot.

Cut flowers and plants from all over the world are for sale in the flower market on the Singel. Those that are not grown in Holland come from Aalsmeer, where many foreign flower growers sell their products at the biggest flower auction in the world. One bizarre consequence of this trade is that mimosas from the south of France are auctioned in Aalsmeer and then, in addition to being sold on the Singel to eager Amsterdammers, exported to Paris.

Some of the sunflowers at the Amsterdam flower market also originate from southern Europe. The Dutch are mad about these sturdy, decorative flowers which bring a bit of sunshine into their homes on rainy days. Japanese tourists recognize the sunflower as one of the favourite subjects of Vincent van Gogh, the one Dutch artist who is perhaps more famous in their homeland than his own.

Art and Administration

Under One Roof

In the 1970s Amsterdam needed two new public buildings: a modern city hall and an opera house. After endless quibbling, particularly over the cost, a unique compromise was reached. The Stopera (a fusion of the Dutch words for city hall, stadhuis, and opera) became two buildings in one. It was completed in two stages, the opera house in 1986 and the city hall in 1988. The building has clean lines broken only by the tall windows and is barren of decoration on the outside. Some Amsterdammers still think the result is a monstrosity; others are quite taken with this marriage of administration and art. The upheaval caused by its construction (for many years, this part of the city was a huge building site) has now been forgotten. Music lovers are happy with the quality of their opera; those needing to visit only the city hall can go in through a separate entrance. The new building has direct access to the Metro station beneath it.

The music and ballet section of the Stopera stands on the bank of the Amstel. Thanks to the high windows spanning two floors, visitors have a splendid view of the river before and after performances. The Amstel ends slightly further down; it used to flow into the IJ behind the Central Station, but the last part of its course was filled in many years ago.

A lamp-post on a bridge over the Amstel, near the Stopera, carries the crown of the Emperor Maximilian of Austria. The privilege of displaying the imperial crown was granted by the Emperor, then ruler of the Low Countries, in 1489. The crown can also be seen in the city's coat of arms and on the spire of the Westertoren.

The foyer, bars and restaurants of the opera house contain many sculptures, mostly inspired by the building's function. One of the most surprising is that of a violinist apparently sinking into the floor. In the entrance of the city hall section, a water column indicates how far under water Amsterdam would be if the Netherlands did not have dunes and dikes.

A second-hand book market is held regularly on the small square to the left of the curved façade. Booksellers from all over the country come to Amsterdam to display their volumes. After the Stopera was completed, houseboats also returned to the Amstel quay.

You can't repress the sense of humour of the stallholders on Waterlooplein. Here, a dummy and two weird-looking dwarves watch over a couple of skinny hemp plants. The dummy is supposed to represent President Clinton wearing an American Drug Enforcement Agency jacket.

You can find old books and atlases on Waterlooplein, but looking for something special is like looking for a needle in a haystack. Most of the books will be in Dutch. Lovers of old books, especially foreign-language books, are better off going to the antiquarian booksellers in the old city centre, a ten-minute walk away.

New 'antiques' compensate for the (near) absence of real ones, as do lots of other pleasing or curious articles which would help create a cosy or unusual interior.

Rummaging in the Waterlooplein market

Among those who loudly protested against the construction of the Stopera in the 1970s were the stallholders of Waterlooplein market. As long as anyone could remember, they had held their daily market here, selling anything from real antiques to rusty tools. With the construction of the Metro and the city hall-cum-opera house, they had to move to an uninspiring square nearby. They have since moved back to part of their old site, but the square and market have lost their original character and the chances of finding an old master these days, amongst all the junk, are next to nothing. Only lovers of odds and ends from grandmother's attic will find much to their taste.

The range of goods on offer at the Waterlooplein market is as wide and colourful as ever, but it has changed in quality. Moulded glassware from the 1950s is displayed next to dolls and cheap silverware; the gilded frames of the paintings are often worth more than the canvases inside them. Further along you might find a flag emblazoned with a portrait of Che Guevara, from the estate of a disappointed Sixties revolutionary.

Jewish History Museum

Before the Second World War, Amsterdam had an important Jewish community. It was established at the end of the 16th century, when many Jews fled from Spanish persecution to the more tolerant Netherlands. This community was cruelly destroyed during the Second World War, when most Dutch Jews were deported to the German concentration camps. After the war, the old Jewish quarter was redeveloped. Of the remaining buildings, the most important are the three synagogues on Jonas Daniël Meijerplein, near the Waterlooplein market. Parts of these house the Joods Historisch Museum. The collections give a rich impression of Jewish historical, cultural and religious life in the Netherlands and of the contribution of the Jewish people to the history of Amsterdam.

The star of David at the entrance to the museum, is formed by two superimposed equilateral triangles.

A lithograph in the museum's collection, drawn in 1861 by Willem Hekking Junior, depicts a scene still easily recognizable today. Hekking was standing on the site of the present-day Jonas Daniël Meijerplein. On the right is the Portuguese Synagogue, which is still in existence. Near the centre is the Moses and Aaron Church (on Waterlooplein) and on the far left are the New and the Great Synagogues that now house the museum.

One of the exhibition rooms in the Joods Historisch Museum contains ritual objects, including menorahs, prayer wheels and prayer cloaks. Part of the collection, assembled under different circumstances in the 1920s, was taken to Germany during the war years. It was found in 1946 and returned to Amsterdam. After moving around for several years, the museum finally found a suitable home here, in the heart of the former Jewish quarter.

Thanks to the relatively recent design, the museum is roomy and well-organized. This room contains part of the collection of ritual objects, including menorahs, prayer wheels and prayer cloaks.

Anne Frank was 11 when this school photo was taken in 1940. Two years later she started writing her diary. It is a moving account of her feelings as a young girl and the fears of the eight people crammed into the secret annexe at the back of Prinsengracht 263. The diary was found in the building after the war. It has not only been published in many languages but also adapted for stage and screen.

Anne Frank house

Until the Second World War, the Anne Frank house on Prinsengracht was a 17th-century canal-side house just like any other. It consisted of a front section, in which the owner lived and had his office, and a rear section used, among other things, for storage. This changed in 1942 after German forces occupied Amsterdam. The front was still used as an office, but a group of Jewish Amsterdammers went into hiding in a secret annexe at the rear of the house, including the families Frank and Van Daan and Mr. Van Dussen – a total of eight people. Despite a number of precautionary measures, such as a revolving bookcase concealing the entrance to the rear of the house, the plan ultimately failed. In August 1944 the residents of the secret annexe were betrayed and arrested. The story of their fearful existence during the two intervening years became world-famous thanks to the diary kept by the young Anne Frank.

The Anne Frank house, with its entrance at Prinsengracht 263, attracts visitors from all over the world. Here they can not only see the rooms where the Jews hid between July 1942 and August 1944, but also discover the wider history of Jewish persecution during the Second World War. Exhibits include hand-written fragments of Anne Frank's diary.

This attic room was part of the secret annexe at the back of the house on Prinsengracht. The living conditions of the eight people hiding in the house have been partly reconstructed. The rest of the building is used by the Anne Frank Foundation as an exhibition centre to keep alive the memory of the Second World War and of the persecution of the Jews.

Renzo Piano's 'shipwreck'

At the point where returning East Indiamen in the 17th century would reef their sails, the hull of a huge ship juts out of the water. A massive disaster has just happened. Survivors are crawling all over the tilting foredeck... This was the imaginative idea for a new building conceived by the Genoese architect and structural engineer, Renzo Piano. Between 1989 and 1997, he turned the idea into reality. The result is the newMetropolis science and technology centre which rises above the entrance to the road tunnel running under the IJ to Amsterdam-Noord. Laid out on four floors, the centre gives an overview of science and technology on the eve of the 21st century. What is so special about the newMetropolis, apart from its shape and concept, is the accessibility of the exhibits. The centre is one big laboratory where the visitor is invited to take an active part in scientific experiments.

A long staircase leads to the roof of the newMetropolis, above the entrance to the IJ tunnel (left). This 'companionway' gives access to the 'promenade deck', a sloping square that Piano designed as a public space where Amsterdammers and tourists could relax. To the left, in the background, is St. Nicholas Church, opposite the Central Station.

At its 'bow' end, the newMetropolis has a restaurant with an open-air terrace. From this high vantage point, visitors have a spectacular view over the centre of Amsterdam. The square in front of the restaurant has a very steep slope which the architect terraced with wide steps. They provide an ideal stage for the street artists who perform here in the summer.

The 'stern' of the newMetropolis rises from the point at which car traffic dives under the IJ on its way to Amsterdam-Noord or the top of Noord-Holland. The walls are clad in oxidized copper. This material not only has low maintenance costs but also highlights the boldness of Renzo Piano's concept, making the newMetropolis a striking successor to one of his earlier public buildings, designed with Richard Rogers: the Pompidou Centre in Paris.

In the 'hold' of the ship, an artificial waterfall provides an insight into the properties of running water. Younger visitors, in particular, are encouraged to participate in numerous projects. These vary from a quick tour of the Internet to laboratory testing of soil samples.

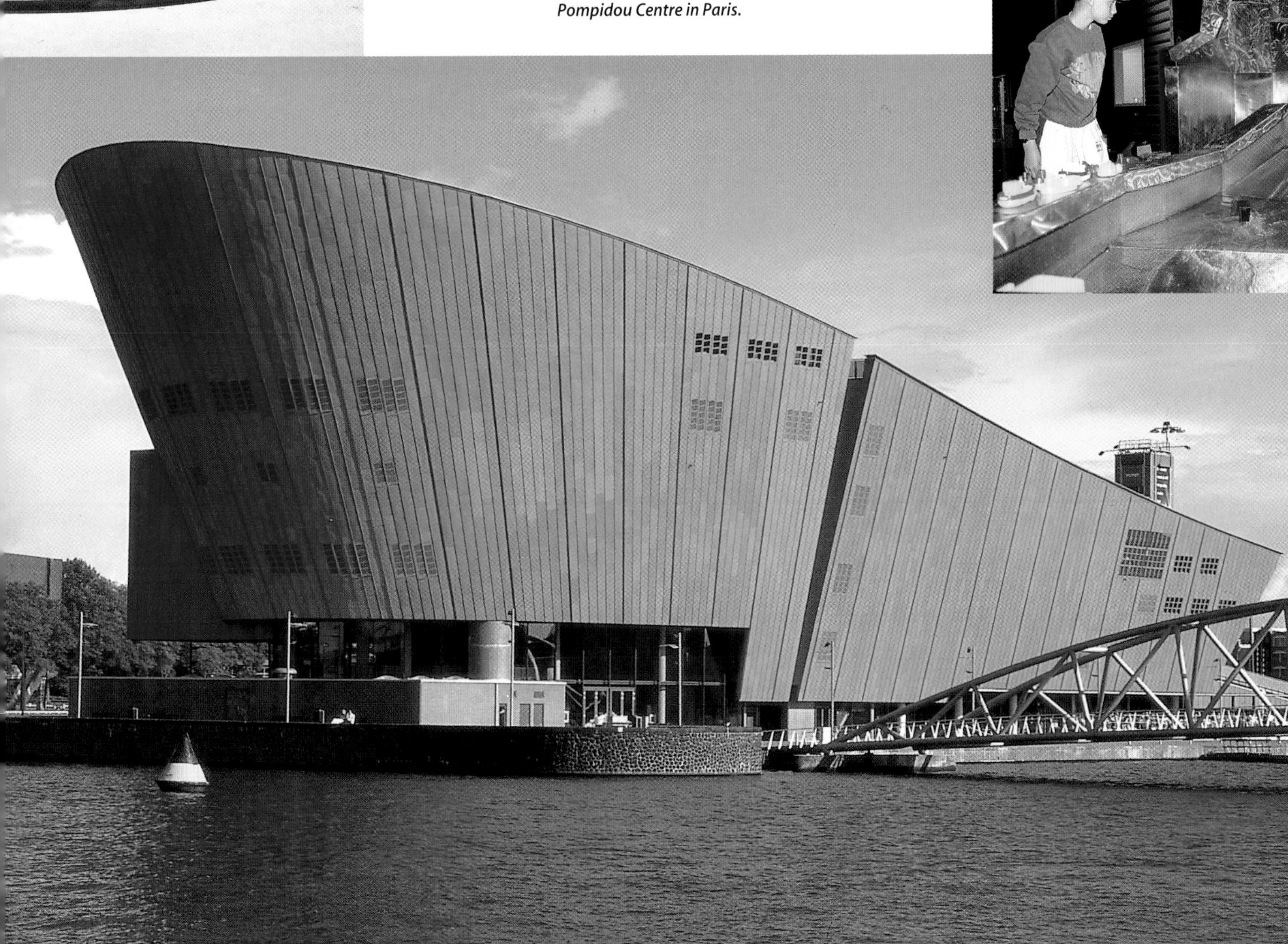

In mid-summer the many, often rare plants growing outside the greenhouses transform the botanical garden into a fragrant sea of colour. Many Amsterdammers come here to enjoy this island of greenery in the middle of the city.

Until the end of the 1980s, the Hortus Botanicus belonged to the University of Amsterdam. Although the garden is now run by a private foundation, the collection of plants still attracts students. In the three-climate conservatory, they can discover many exotic species.

Nature in miniature

Nowhere in the centre of Amsterdam is the city greener than a few hundred metres from the Stopera, Waterlooplein and the Jewish History Museum. Here, within walking distance of each other, are the Artis Zoo and a botanical garden, the Hortus Botanicus. The Hortus was established in the 17th century and benefited from colonial expansion. Dutch merchantmen brought back plants from all over the world which were completely new to the botanists of the time. At the end of the 1980s, cutbacks threatened to close the centuries-old garden, but a fund-raising campaign among the people of Amsterdam saved it. Not only was the Hortus kept open; in 1993 it even gained a new conservatory. Around 10,000 species of plants grow inside and outside this enormous glass palace, from tiny ferns to towering palms.

The new conservatory in the Hortus Botanicus has three climates under one roof: tropical, sub-tropical and desert. Visitors – numbering around 65,000 a year – can view the plants on the ground floor or from a number of high walkways. The Hortus has three other greenhouses that are open to the public.

Opposite the main conservatory is an old orangery where tropical and sub-tropical plants used to be housed during the winter. It has now been converted into a tea-room.

Like the Zuiderkerk, the Westerkerk was built by Hendrick de Keyser. It was clearly designed for Protestant worship: the focus of the bare, white interior is not a main altar but a pulpit. Rembrandt is said to be buried in the church. Unfortunately, no one knows where.

The wooden Amstel Church on Amstelveld was built in 1670 as a makeshift church for the Protestants. It was intended to be replaced by a stone church, but the plan never materialized and the temporary building was never torn down. Over the years it has been used for all sorts of purposes, from stables to a drill hall. Still a Protestant church, the building also houses a restaurant, with an inviting terrace on the square that was once reserved for its stone replacement.

The steeple of the Zuiderkerk (South Church) towers over the houses along the canal. The church was built at the start of the 17th century and was the first large Protestant church in the country. The church itself is no longer used as a place of worship and is closed to the public. However, it is possible to climb the tower, and those that do are rewarded with a magnificent view of the old town and the IJ. Bell-ringers regularly perform on the Zuiderkerk's carillon.

The piety of the merchant

In its eight centuries, Amsterdam has never had a reputation as a pious city. Only one small miracle has been recorded here: in 1343 an invalid vomited a consecrated communion wafer into the fire in his sick-room. The next day it was found undamaged among the ashes in the hearth. In this city of trade, it is no surprise that the historic churches testify more to the status-seeking character of its rich merchants than to their devotion. Most of the large churches were built after the Protestants took over the city at the end of the 16th century. In many cases the influence of the Reformation is undetectable from the outside: Amsterdam's master builders would not break with tradition so easily. Inside, however, there can be no doubt about the change in religious temper: bare white walls, no altar, pulpit and organ substituting as the central focus. The earliest place of worship in the city is the Old Church in the middle of the red-light district. It was built around 1300 and a Renaissance-style extension was added two centuries later.

The famous organ of the Westerkerk (West Church)is one of those that were rebuilt or greatly increased in size after Catholic worship was forbidden in Amsterdam at the end of the 16th century. Once the organ became a central focus as churches were stripped of graven images, it needed extra grandeur in order to provide a fitting accompaniment to the pious hymns of the Protestant believers.

The oasis of the pious women

Beguines were an innovation of the 12th century: pious women who lived a sort of convent life, centred around a courtyard, without taking vows as nuns. From the 14th century, Amsterdam had a beguinage called the Begijnhof. It is still there, although the beguines are not and the little courtyard is no longer on the edge of town but close to the city's bustling shopping district around the Dam. A small gate leads to an oasis of peace that no one would expect to find here. The (Catholic) beguines were allowed to remain here after the Reformation. However, they had to turn over their church to the Scottish Presbyterians. From 1665 onwards, they worshipped in a secret chapel opposite the 'English church'. This chapel is still in existence, hidden behind an ordinary façade.

Amsterdam's beguinage does not have the medieval character of those in the south of the Netherlands and Flanders. The narrow houses are built in a style typical of the 17th and 18th centuries, with every type of façade that can be found along the canals.

A stone beguine commemorates the life of the lay sisters of Amsterdam. Not far from this statue is the gravestone of a beguine who died in 1654. She wished to be buried not in the church but 'in the gutter'. This was her way of atoning for the fact that her family had turned from Catholicism during the Reformation.

Since 1607, the Begijnhofskerk (Beguinage Church) has been in the hands of the Presbyterians. This 'English church' is still in use today, like the secret chapel that was established for the beguines in a house opposite.

History of a city

Amsterdam grew from its origins as a fishing village on the Amstel, established around 1270, into one of the richest cities of the 17th-century world. It went on to become the capital of a small country. This long and not always comfortable history can be surveyed in a couple of hours in the Amsterdams Historisch Museum. It is located in the city's former orphanage, established in the 17th century. The main entrance is on Kalverstraat, one of the shopping streets leading to the Dam. In the restored complex, eight centuries of Amsterdam life are displayed in maps, models, panoramas, paintings, sculptures, clothing and utensils.

One of the most impressive sections of the museum is the Schuttersgalerij (Musketeer's Gallery). Located in a covered passageway over a filled-in ditch, it houses a number of group portraits of the city's civil watch in the 17th century. These large canvases, though painted by lesser masters, invite comparison with Rembrandt's famous Night Watch, *which hangs in the Rijksmuseum (see page 71).*

Looking at the group portraits in the Schuttersgalerij, one cannot fail to be impressed by the superior quality of Rembrandt's portrayal of the musketeers in the Rijksmuseum. Like these paintings, his Night Watch *was a commercial commission: he made his living from this type of work. But the way in which he captured a company of the civil watch on canvas, with so much movement and detail, is a world away from these stiff portraits turned out by his colleagues.*

The entrance to the museum is a gate dating from 1581, which used to be part of another building. In the 17th century, images of eight orphans were added around the orphanage's crest, a dove. The motto dates from 1634. Written by Joost van den Vondel, one of the Netherlands' greatest poets, it asks passers-by to make a contribution to the orphans' upkeep.

A number of 16th-century breastplates are cleverly displayed in a cabinet outside the Amsterdam Historical Museum. If you squint, you can see a platoon of halberdiers marching to the walls to defend their city.

This huge statue of the giant Goliath dominates the museum's restaurant. It was carved from one tree trunk and used to be part of a maze on Prinsengracht, as did the smaller statues at its feet. In its day, the giant could move its head and roll its eyes.

To the left of a café in the museum complex are the lockers in which the orphans used to store their toys.

GY MOET DE BALLEN RAKEN EN NIET HET LAKEN

A sign-writer puts the finishing touches to the window of De Twee Zwaantjes (The Two Swans) café on Prinsengracht. Amsterdam has thousands of cafés like this, often with quirky names such as De Drie Anna's (The Three Annas), De Blaffende Vis (The Barking Fish) or Het Snorretje (The Little Moustache). You can always get a drink, including spirits, and often snacks and bar meals. Occasionally there is a billiard table, and, in a few cafés in the city centre, Amsterdammers can indulge their love of opera and operetta.

You can usually find a café or a place to eat, even in the smallest alleyways such as in the Gebed zonder Eind (Endless Prayer), near the university.

Amsterdam has become a city of pavement cafés. The sun only has to shine for a second and tables and chairs appear in even the smallest streets in the city centre as if by magic.

The classic Dutch interior of De Oude Taveerne (The Old Tavern) whisks you back into the past. This pub on Durgerdammerdijk, north of the IJ, is 200 years old.

Temple to Lady Fortune

Gambling was illegal in the Netherlands until well after the Second World War. No casinos, no football pools, no lotto, not even a flutter on the (infrequent) horse races. Only the national lottery was permitted, because the government could earn money from that itself.

Gradually the rules were relaxed. Roulette and other games of are now allowed, though carefully licensed. The only legal casinos are operated by Holland Casinos, and this company is monitored very closely. It has built a luxurious gambling palace in Amsterdam, complete with gaming rooms, bars and restaurants.

The luxurious entrance to the Amsterdam casino sets the tone for the rest of the building, which attempts to recreate – in a modern way – the atmosphere of the old-style casinos of Nice and Monte Carlo.

The back of the casino has a fine curved façade which looks out over the Leidsegracht. In the background is the American Hotel, one of the grand hotels built in Amsterdam at the begenning of the 20th century. It has been a listed building since 1972.

In the large gaming room in the Amsterdam casino you can play roulette and card games such as blackjack. If this gambling temple does not suit you, you can try your luck on slot machines. The entrance to the casino is on Max Euweplein, a new square close to the municipal theatre. It is ironic, that Euwe was anything but a gambler. He was a mathematician who in 1935 beat Alexander Alekhine to become chess world champion.

CONCERT-GEBOUW
25, 26, 27 mei
The Philadelphia Orchestra Festival
Wolfgang Sawallisch
Frank Peter Zimmermann

The Amsterdam Concertgebouw was built on what a hundred years ago was the southern edge of the city. The architect, A. L. van Gendt, was proud of the fact that he could build in any style the customer wanted. The customer wanted neo-classical, and that's what he got.

Musical extremes

Is Amsterdam a musical city? Sometimes you might think so, especially if you are walking in the Jordaan, a district from which many popular singers have emerged. From time to time the cafés open their doors for every true Amsterdammer to demonstrate, like a miniature Pavarotti or Callas, that he or she missed fame and fortune by a whisker. The many barrel organs heard playing their popular melodies on sunny days belong to the same tradition. At the other extreme is the world-famous Royal Concertgebouw Orchestra. Its home is in the Amsterdam Concertgebouw, a neo-classical concert hall dating from the end of the 19th century.

An Amsterdam barrel organ exhibits the rich, unsubtle decoration characteristic of such instruments. The figurines represent musicians. Usually they are connected to the machinery and 'play' their instruments in time with the music. The back of the organ is open, and you can see how the tunes are created from an 'organ book' full of punched holes. The organ grinders collect money from the public in a copper tin.

The Rijksmuseum is so big that there is no point in 'checking it out between lunch and dinner'. The best thing to do is to select and concentrate on what you really want to see.

Viewed from the side, the two towers that dominate the Rijksmuseum appear at their most Gothic. Many Protestants felt the building was far too Catholic in style, including King William III, who never set foot in it for this reason.

THE RIJKSMUSEUM

The Rijksmuseum houses the largest collection of art in the Netherlands. Each year, it attracts more than a million visitors. They mainly come to see the unique collection of Dutch masters of the 17th century, such as Frans Hals, Jan Steen, Johannes Vermeer, Jacob van Ruysdael and, most of all, Rembrandt van Rijn. His *Night Watch*, a commissioned portrait of a company of the Amsterdam civil watch, would seem to be the central attraction for most visitors. It is not by any means the best work of this talented miller's son from Leiden, but thanks to the energy, the Rembrandtesque clair-obscur and the size of the painting (it has a room to itself), it is very much the main work in the Rijksmuseum.

Among the other great masterpieces from the Golden Age are four fabulous Vermeers. And anyone wishing to see what life was like in old Holland will greatly enjoy the Dutch genre painters, Jan Steen in particular. He is best known for his everyday scenes, of happy groups of people celebrating, of families around a table, of friends in a pub. The scenes in his paintings are often exuberant, noisy and messy, which explains the Dutch expression 'having a home like Jan Steen's'. The most recent paintings in the collection are from the 19th century. In more than 250 rooms, there is also a wide variety of other exhibits, ranging from etchings and drawings, an impressive collection of Asian art, glass and silverware, beautiful doll's houses from the 19th century, Delft blue ware and porcelain, costumes, and an illustrated history of the Netherlands.

Anyone who thinks they have spotted a similarity between the Rijksmuseum and the Central Station is quite correct. Both were designed by P. J. H. Cuypers. This Roman Catholic architect from the 19th century was a student of the Frenchman Eugène Viollet-le-Duc, the founding father of the Gothic Revival.

At the start of the 17th century, artists began to discover the picturesque in the Dutch landscape. They painted it with great realism and attention to detail. One of the masters of the genre was Hendrick Avercamp. His winter landscape from around 1608 depicts a huge number of minute details, from the clothing of the time to a game that may have been a forerunner of ice hockey. There are more ice-scapes to be seen in the Rijksmuseum, painted among others by one of Avercamp's near contemporaries, Aart van der Neer. Famous names from the 19th century include Koekkoek, Schelfhout and Leickert; you can find their works in the south wing of the museum.

One well known and popular picture in the Rijksmuseum is The Kitchen-Maid *by Johannes Vermeer, painted in around 1660. Its power lies primarily in the light, which enters through the window and plays magically on the figure and the objects in the room. Centuries later, photographers would use this technique to give their images depth and dimension.*

Rembrandt's Night Watch *shows a company of Amsterdam musketeers who are on the point of marching off. The captain – dressed in black – is clearly giving the command and has already started moving himself: the heel of his left foot is rising. The drummer at the right of the painting is beating his drum. In most portraits of musketeers – compare the* Night Watch *with the works in the musketeer's gallery in the Amsterdam Historical Museum on page 57 – the figures are perfectly posed. Rembrandt, on the other hand, shows a lively, chaotic scene. He painted an instant in time, and the dramatic lighting emphasized the action.*

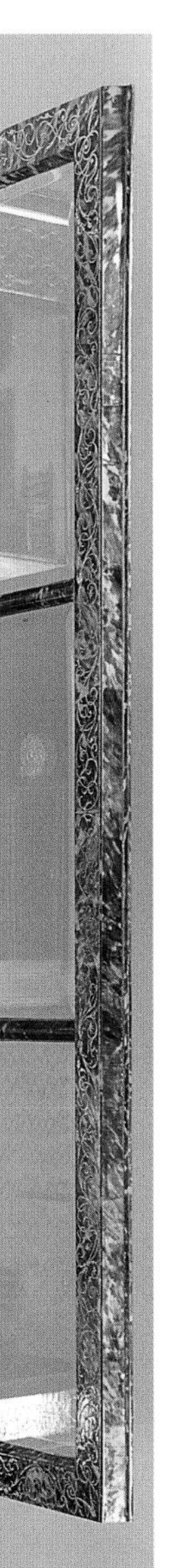

The collection of doll's houses in the Rijksmuseum is extremely popular, and not only with children. They were not intended to be children's toys, but showpieces of the cabinet-maker's art. This piece is the most splendid in the collection. It represents the interior of a house from the 17th century. The walls and ceiling of the large living room are painted with landscapes and birds; there is porcelain crockery in the kitchen and the miniature books in the library contain real text. The chair from this house, shown above, reveals the loving attention its maker paid to even the smallest of details.

The historical department of the museum contains a number of scale models of ships. This is the oldest known model of an East Indiaman, a merchant vessel of the East India Company. It dates from 1651 and is a model of the Prins Willem, *a ship that was launched a year earlier. The historical department has much to offer, even to those who are not Dutch, since the history of the Netherlands overlapped with the history of other countries. For example, one topic of the exhibition is the Dutch presence on the Japanese island of Deshima, near Nagasaki. There is a grand painting of the Battle of Waterloo by J. W. Pieneman, and for the more contemporary-minded, many aspects of modern Dutch society are illustrated in photographs.*

An East Indiaman braves the terrors of the deep in this scene on a 17th-century plate. Much of the crockery of the period records the triumphs and tribulations of the passage to the East Indies.

The collection of paintings in the Rijksmuseum includes pictures from medieval to modern times. Two important painters from the 19th century, whose work is represented in the collection, are Isaac Israels and George Breitner. Both belonged to the Amsterdam School. Israels spent a great deal of time in France, and was influenced by Post-Impressionism, as can be seen in this scene, Donkey riding along the beach, *which demonstrates Israels' lightness of brush stroke and his liking for cheerful colours. Breitner painted Amsterdam as it was at the turn of the century. The way he managed to suggest movement in his paintings is shown in* The Singel Bridge near Paleisstraat. *The action is driven by the figure in the foreground, who seems to be walking out of the picture.*

In the work of both Breitner and Israels, we see snapshots of everyday life. Israels liked to paint portraits of sophisticated women or, as shown here, well dressed city children. Breitner preferred the dynamics of the big city, mainly Amsterdam. He painted city life in all weathers, including snow, sleet or drizzle.

THE PAST FOR SALE

Directly opposite the entrance to the Rijksmuseum and across three bridges lies Nieuwe Spiegelstraat. For many years, this short street has been known to enthusiasts from around the world as the centre of Amsterdam's antique trade. You can buy antiques in other parts of the city, but many of the shops on Nieuwe Spiegelstraat are somewhat less daunting. The proximity of the Rijksmuseum probably helps. You step from one museum into another, as it were – the difference being that everything behind these windows is for sale.

For anyone not looking for a specific piece, antique shops like this are a paradise to rummage around in. There is something for everyone: globes, toy trains, grandfather clocks, binoculars, statuettes, mirrors and bric-à-brac. Most of the pieces are original in mint condition and therefore not cheap.

One or two of the shops on Nieuwe Spiegelstraat specialize in old Dutch tiles. This is not obvious from the tasteful composition of mirror, chandelier and bouquet displayed in the window. At the back of the shop, however, the visitor can choose from hundreds of tiles with which the Dutch used to decorate their houses.

Antique shops like this, specializing in furniture, used to fill Nieuwe Spiegelstraat. This is where connoisseurs come to find an 18th-century cabinet, a Gobelin or a Louis XV chair. These shops do not invite you to come in and walk around. Sometimes, you even have to ring the bell.

That antiques are for sale elsewhere in the city is shown by this shop window in Langebrugsteeg, in the old city centre. Here we find a dealer specializing in gold, silver and jewellery. Of course, the most precious pieces are not in the shop window, but locked in the safe.

The warehouse of the golden carriage.

The grass mower.

In the old fortification.

The glowing oven.

Advertising from centuries ago

In the old part of Amsterdam, pedestrians constantly come across colourful plaques set in the walls. Sometimes they are at the top of the façade, other times between the windows. There are an awful lot of them, and from their condition it is obvious that they must be cherished. These plaques have long since lost their purpose, however. They date mainly from the 16th, 17th and 18th centuries and served to identify the houses in Amsterdam before they had numbers. Some bear the name of the house or of its inhabitants at the time, others depict a craft or trade and functioned as a shop sign. Plaques also often show a year, usually the date when the building was completed. The plaques that remain are only a fraction of the many that used to exist.

The red oil mill.

Markets of Amsterdam

Amsterdam would not be a city if it did not have its open-air markets. It still has a few specialist markets, such as the flower market on the Singel, the flea market on Waterlooplein and the stamp market behind the Amsterdam Historical Museum, though the Ossenmarkt (Ox Market) has long since disappeared. In addition, it boasts a number of markets selling a wider range of goods from fresh fruit and vegetables to clothes and books. The best known, which has become a tourist attraction, is the market in Albert Cuypstraat.

A market is held each Saturday on Noordermarkt, at the foot of the 17th-century Noorderkerk (North Church). Some of the stalls sell books, second-hand but seldom antiquarian. A few metres to the left is the 'farmer's market', with dozens of stalls selling organic produce. This ranges from fruit that looks very ecologically correct to a wide variety of mushrooms and loaves of bread containing so many different whole grains that they are almost too heavy to lift.

The pedlar loudly hawking his wares in a broad Amsterdam accent and with a sharp sense of humour has largely disappeared. Some of the stallholders have not lost their sense of visual humour, however. High above a stall in the Dappermarkt, a line-up of cancan dancers' legs makes a play for attention, drawing the eye to a display of lingerie and hosiery.

On most market days, there is a vast range of fresh food on offer in the city, from fruit to fish, game and poultry. Many Amsterdammers do their daily shopping in these markets. Apart from food, there is a lot of clothing for sale, as well as tools, cheap watches, even cheaper trinkets and whatever else the market traders have on offer.

Second-hand – and also antiquarian – books can be bought all over Amsterdam, for example in this market on Spui, a side street off Kalverstraat.

Vase with Sunflowers dates from 1889, when Van Gogh was living in Arles. He made a number of paintings of sunflowers during this period. In the 1980s, these fetched huge sums at auctions around the world. Questions are now being asked as to whether Van Gogh painted all of them.

Crows in a Wheatfield from 1890 is one of the last canvases painted by Van Gogh during his stay in southern France and reflects the artist's state of mind during the final months of his life. The sunny colours used during his happier years have made way for more sombre tones.

Vincent van Gogh in Amsterdam

When Vincent van Gogh died in 1890, a significant part of his work was owned by his brother, Theo. His son, Ir. V. W. van Gogh, presented this important legacy to the Dutch nation on one condition: that a separate museum must be built for it. Around 200 of the artist's paintings and 500 of his drawings have been on display here since 1973. They range from his earliest work, sombre canvases of which The Potato Eaters is the most famous, to the tormented works of his final months in Auvers-sur-Oise. The collection is exhibited on three floors. It also includes Van Gogh's collection of 19th-century Japanese prints and a small number of canvases by contemporaries such as Gauguin, Toulouse-Lautrec, Bernard and Monet.

Visitors pass through one of the rooms in the Van Gogh Museum. In terms of functionality, form and use of space, the interior clearly bears the stamp of its architect, Rietveld. The stark Bauhaus appearance of the building dramatically clashes with that of the two other museums on Museumplein.

The Van Gogh Museum on Paulus Potterstraat is one of the three large museums on Museumplein, the others being the neighbouring Stedelijk Museum and the Rijksmuseum. The plans were the work of Gerrit Rietveld, a prominent architect and furniture designer from the De Stijl group (of which other more internationally famous artists were members, among them Mondrian and Van Doesburg). The functional building, completed nine years after the architect's death, houses the largest collection of Van Goghs in the world.

Modern art behind old walls

From the outside you see a sumptuous neo-Renaissance building. If you did not know what lies behind this 1895 façade, you would never guess. In fact, within these brick walls is the Stedelijk Museum containing the most important collection of modern and contemporary art in the country, and one of the most remarkable galleries of its kind in Europe. Its fame dates from just after the Second World War when two consecutive directors, Willem Sandberg and Edy de Wilde, cleared out a large part of the existing collection. They and their successors implemented a purchasing policy that created a permanent collection covering the whole range of 20th-century art, especially post-1945. It contains paintings, sculptures, drawings, prints, photographs and applied art and streches from Matisse to Koons, to name two extremes. The Stedelijk has gained international fame for its continually changing exhibitions mirroring the latest trends.

The restaurant and café of the Stedelijk Museum overlook an ornamental lake. One of the most remarkable objects in the garden is a work by kinetic artist Jean Tinguely. His sculpture, and virtually everything in the museum, is in stark contrast with the original building, part of which is just visible.

The next call *is a work by the painter and printer Hendrik Nicolaas Werkman, whose reputation has spread beyond the Netherlands. He is known for a series of prints inspired by the Chassidic Legends of the German philosopher Martin Buber.* The next call *was also a magazine Werkman published, with typography influenced by the Russian constructivists.*

One of the large rooms in the Stedelijk shows what has been achieved by the post-war directors. One effect of their dynamic policy is that parts of the permanent collection never stay long in the same place.

Suprematism *is one of a series of paintings by Kazimir Malevich. The Stedelijk owns a large collection of work by this internationally acclaimed Russian artist, one of the great pioneers of early 20th-century art, including 29 paintings as well as drawings and gouaches. The one reproduced here is a beautiful example of Malevich's pursuit of pure shapes.*

The ornamentation on the museum's staircase shows that the building was never intended for work by artists such as Mondrian, Appel, Warhol and Polke. Although the director Willem Sandberg made radical changes to the interior after 1945 (he had all the walls painted white, for example), he did not touch the marble balustrade. His 'storm of images' had already caused enough indignation.

Although Amsterdam's maritime importance has declined, the city still has a Naval College. Students are trained in electronics, satellite navigation and other subjects that their predecessors in the 17th century would never have dreamed of. Some old traditions are kept up, however. Sometimes, the boys take to the oars and row their longboat at Olympic speed through the canals.

AMSTERDAM AND WATER

Thanks to its canals, Amsterdam became known as the Venice of the North, and thanks to its fleet it was the most powerful city in 17th-century Holland. The fleet has gone. The warships of the Dutch Royal Navy are moored in Den Helder and the container ships and tankers of the modern merchant fleet are based in Rotterdam. But the canals are still here, the domain of canal-trip boats, pedalos, water taxis and the odd Amsterdammer wanting to mess about in a boat. There are small marinas along the canals where people can moor their boats or lay them up for the winter.

An extraordinarily picturesque marina can be found at Westelijke Eilanden (Western Islands), a district of Amsterdam approximately one kilometre to the west of the Central Station. There was the scent of pitch and tar here as long ago as the 17th century. When serious soil contamination was discovered a few years ago, it turned out that most of it dated from that time. What makes this vista so special is not just the wooden bascule bridges that connect two of the three islands, but the row of façades along Zandhoek.

Since the 1960s, the Municipal Transport Company has made it a custom to paint some of the Amsterdam trams with decorative designs. To some extent, the motive was commercial: advertising brought in money. However, playfulness and creativity also played a part. Some trams have been turned into moving canvases, either because someone had a bright idea for a design or an artist was let loose on the carriages. What visitors forget to photograph one year will not be around the next.

Tram 2 is an ordinary Amsterdam streetcar, seen here with an attractive backdrop: the Leidsestraat, a shopping street between Flower Market and the bustling Leidseplein.

Public Transport

Amsterdammers have nothing to complain about when it comes to public transport – although they love to do so. The city can be reached by train from every direction. There are eleven railway stations, from the opulent Central Station to the almost transparent Sloterdijk and Duivendrecht stations. Underground trains carry passengers to the furthest suburbs and to Amstelveen; in the city itself, a fine-mesh network of trams and local buses carries passengers as close as possible to where they want to be. Regional buses serve towns in the surrounding rural areas. And then there are the many taxis ready for use night and day. Public transport on the water, as in Venice, has often been considered but has never really taken off, maybe because Amsterdam has always had more streets than canals.

Sloterdijk, at the western edge of the city, is one of the newest stations in Amsterdam. Together with Duivendrecht station, this light and airy building completed the rail ring round the capital. The platforms are on two different levels. Both stations have Metro, tram and local bus connections. Unlike the older stations, they have substantial car-parks.

Bank as fairy-tale palace

When the head office of ING Bank went up in the new town of Amsterdam Zuidoost in 1987, few Amsterdammers knew what to think of it. Some saw it as a monstrosity, while others were reminded of a fairy-tale palace or modern fortress. In fact, the brick-clad colossus was built on the basis of two guiding principles: low energy consumption and the anthroposophic idea that architecture should follow the rules of nature. The first principle was achieved primarily by the shape, in which right angles are virtually eliminated and the greatest possible surface area is exposed to the sun's rays. The second prompted the pentagons, one of which tops the middle tower.

On one side, this chimera of a building rises through one of the busiest and most modern shopping centres in the city, the Amsterdamse Poort. The cosmopolitan crowds using this centre reflect Amsterdam's welcoming attitude to people of many nationalities who have made the city their home in the past few decades.

The fairy-tale castle was built in an S shape. Its asymmetrical design was not just a creative idea on the part of the two architects, A. Alberts and M. van Huut, but arose from meticulous calculations to establish the most energy-efficient profile.

The playing field of the immense ArenA is not at ground level but on the first floor above the Transferium, a parking space for approximately 2,000 cars. This unusual design initially caused a few problems. The grass had difficulty rooting in the artificial ground and could only be kept in good condition for the whole season with a lot of hard work and ingenuity. It is therefore covered over when used for events other than football matches.

The Ajax Amsterdam stadium, built at a cost of 290 million guilders (£100 million), nestles between the new tower blocks of the Zuidoost district. The architect, Rob Schuurman, designed the ArenA as a multi-purpose building that could be used for concerts and mass meetings as well as football matches. In contrast with older stadiums, ArenA has no terraces; there are comfortable bucket seats for the 51,000 spectators. The intention is to create a new night-life complex around the ArenA, starting with a large multiplex cinema.

Spaceship for Ajax Amsterdam

By the mid-1980s, Ajax Amsterdam had already enjoyed an international reputation for many years. It had a collection of cups of every shape and size, produced such players as Cruijff, Van Basten, Gullit and Rijkaard and had an attacking, attractive style that drew big crowds. The only thing missing was a stadium fit for international fixtures.

The original home of Ajax in Watergraafsmeer may have been holy ground for many of the club's supporters, but the club had long outgrown it. For big matches they had to use the Olympic Stadium, built in 1928. These inadequate facilities became history on 14th August 1996, when Ajax played AC Milan at the inauguration of the Amsterdam ArenA. This hyper-modern, covered stadium in the Zuidoost district looks like a spaceship that has landed suddenly in the polder. The sliding roof has an area of 33,650 m^2 in two sections, both of which can be opened or closed in twenty minutes.

For special events at night the ArenA has, in addition to the normal floodlights, an illumination system designed by a lighting artist.

Schiphol

In 1917 a military airfield was constructed near Fortress Schiphol and in 1920 it was opened to civil aviation. Had anyone predicted that by the end of the century the airport would be handling some 350,000 flights a year, it would surely have been given a name that foreigners could pronounce. Most visitors say 'Skiphol', but that does not make them any less welcome.

Nearly 28 million passengers, more than a million tons of freight and 41,000 tons of mail pass through Schiphol every year. These are amazing figures for a country as small as the Netherlands and Schiphol is of great importance to the Dutch economy. It also provides vital export facilities to the nearby Aalsmeer flower auction.

Schiphol is the home of KLM (Royal Dutch Airlines), one of the most successful airlines in the world. That, too, is curious when you consider the small size of its home market. That KLM – not the only Dutch airline – should have grown as it has is down to quality and enterprise, the same characteristics that made the Dutch East India Company such a powerful commercial force in the 17th century.

Martinair
EXIT-1

Amsterdam is published by Inmerc bv, Wormer, the Netherlands

The following people worked on this book:
Photography: Jan den Hengst and others (see photo credits)
Text: Jacques Constant
Translation: Babel, Utrecht
Art direction: Loek de Leeuw
Design: Pieter Klomp
Editing and production: Inmerc bv, Wormer
Final editing: Simon Rigge

Photo credits:
Almost all the photographs for this book were taken by Jan den Hengst.
The following also provided photos:
Amsterdam Airport Schiphol
Amsterdam ArenA
Anne Frank Stichting
Benelux Press
Joods Historisch Museum
newMetropolis
Rijksmuseum Foundation
Stedelijk Museum
Van Gogh Museum

This book has been published in eight languages:

Dutch:	ISBN 90 6611 305 7
English:	ISBN 90 6611 325 1
French:	ISBN 90 6611 335 9
German:	ISBN 90 6611 315 4
Spanish:	ISBN 90 6611 355 3
Italian:	ISBN 90 6611 345 6
Russian:	ISBN 90 6611 365 0
Japanese:	ISBN 90 6611 375 8

ISBN 90 6611 325 1 NUGI 672